EDGE BOOKS™

DRAWING COOL STUFF

HOW TO DRAW

COMIC HEROES

by Aaron Sautter

illustrated by Cynthia Martin

Capstone
press®

Mankato, Minnesota

Edge Books are published by Capstone Press,
151 Good Counsel Drive, P.O. Box 669, Mankato, Minnesota 56002.
www.capstonepress.com

Library of Congress Cataloging-in-Publication Data
Sautter, Aaron.
   How to draw comic heroes / by Aaron Sautter; illustrated by Cynthia Martin.
   p. cm.—(Edge books. Drawing cool stuff)
   Includes bibliographical references and index.
   Summary: "Lively text and fun illustrations describe how to draw mighty comic
heroes"—Provided by publisher.
   ISBN–13: 978-1-4296-0074-3 (hardcover)
   ISBN–10: 1-4296-0074-8 (hardcover)
   1. Heroes in art—Juvenile literature. 2. Cartooning—Technique—Juvenile
literature. I. Martin, Cynthia, 1961– II. Title. III. Series.
NC1764.8.H47S28 2008
741.5—dc22   2007003450

Credits
Jason Knudson, designer

1 2 3 4 5 6 12 11 10 09 08 07

TABLE OF CONTENTS

WELCOME!

You probably picked this book because you love comic book heroes. Or you picked it because you like to draw. Whatever the reason, get ready to dive into the world of comic heroes!

Heroes in comic books do all kinds of amazing things. Most heroes have at least one superpower. They can fly, turn invisible, or have super strength. But all comic book heroes have one thing in common—they always get the bad guy in the end.

This book is just a starting point. Once you've learned how to draw the different heroic characters in this book, you can start drawing your own. Let your imagination run wild, and see what sort of mighty heroes you can create!

To get started, you'll need some supplies:

1. First you'll need drawing paper. Any type of blank, unlined paper will do.

2. Pencils are the easiest to use for your drawing projects. Make sure you have plenty of them.

3. You have to keep your pencils sharp to make clean lines. Keep a pencil sharpener close by. You'll use it a lot.

4. As you practice drawing, you'll need a good eraser. Pencil erasers wear out very fast. Get a rubber or kneaded eraser. You'll be glad you did.

5. When your drawing is finished, you can trace over it with a black ink pen or thin felt-tip marker. The dark lines will really make your work stand out.

6. If you decide to color your drawings, colored pencils and markers usually work best. You can also use colored pencils to shade your drawings and make them more lifelike.

MR. DYNAMO

Mr. Dynamo has the strength of 50 men and is nearly indestructible. He can smash through brick walls and knock thugs silly with a single punch. He is the head of his own crime-fighting family, Team Dynamo.

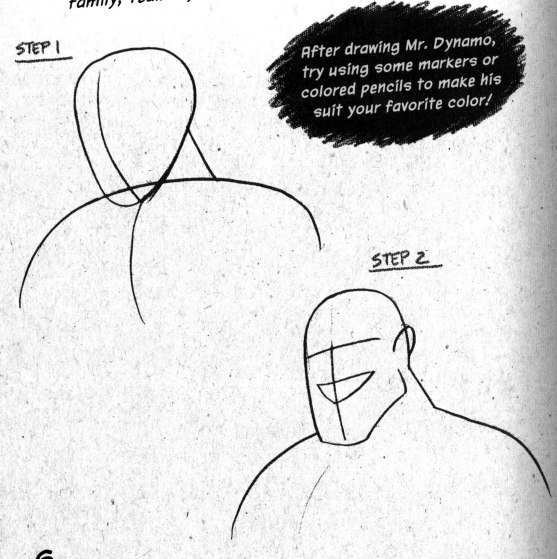

After drawing Mr. Dynamo, try using some markers or colored pencils to make his suit your favorite color!

STEP 1

STEP 2

STEP 3

STEP 4

FINAL!

7

MRS. DYNAMO

Mrs. Dynamo can teleport through walls and make crooks tell the truth. When she met Mr. Dynamo, she fell in love and decided to start a new crime-fighting career. She's now an important part of Team Dynamo.

STEP 1

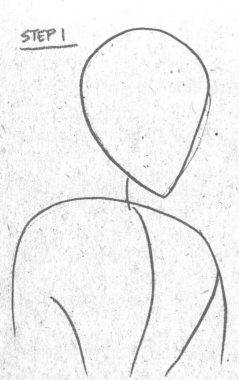

After drawing Mrs. Dynamo, try making your own female hero with a different costume or hairstyle!

STEP 2

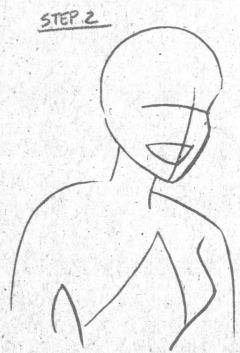

STEP 3

STEP 4

FINAL!

9

DEBBIE DYNAMO

Debbie Dynamo is the most gifted of the entire Dynamo family. She is the only one who can fly. She can also create bolts of lightning out of thin air. With training, the Dynamos think she can be a strong force for good when she grows up.

When you're done with this drawing, try it again with lightning shooting from Debbie's fists!

STEP 1

STEP 2

STEP 3

STEP 4

FINAL!

11

DANNY DYNAMO

Danny Dynamo is the youngest member of Team Dynamo. He's not as strong as his dad, but he can already stop a car in its tracks! He recently discovered that he can teleport himself over short distances, just like his mom.

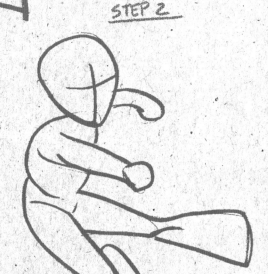

STEP 1

When you're done with this drawing, try showing Danny holding back a crook's getaway car!

STEP 2

STEP 3

STEP 4

FINAL!

13

TEAM DYNAMO

As a team, the Dynamos have caught hundreds of thieves, muggers, and other thugs. They've also helped put away several major crime bosses. Along with their trusted family pet, Mighty Mutt, this hero team is feared by criminals around the world.

Once you've mastered Team Dynamo, try drawing them in action! What sorts of criminals would you like to see them fight?

STEP 1

STEP 2

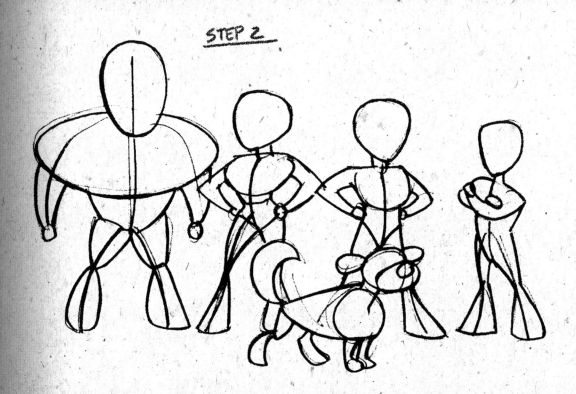

STEP 3

TO FINISH THIS DRAWING,
TURN TO THE NEXT PAGE!

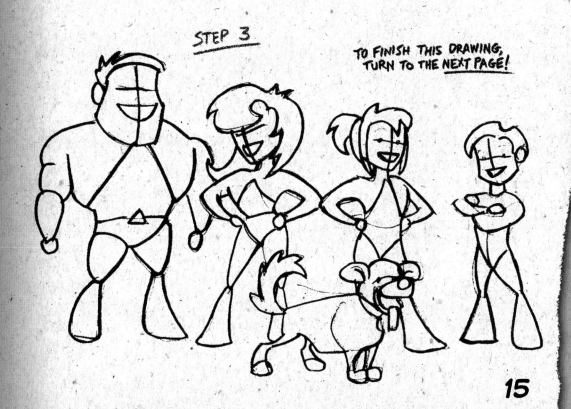

STEP 4

STEP 5

FINAL!

STRETCH

People gave Bill the nickname of Stretch because he was so tall and skinny. He discovered his powers while playing a baseball game. On a long hit, he reached out and caught it over the fence—from third base! Stretch has used his ability to fight crime ever since.

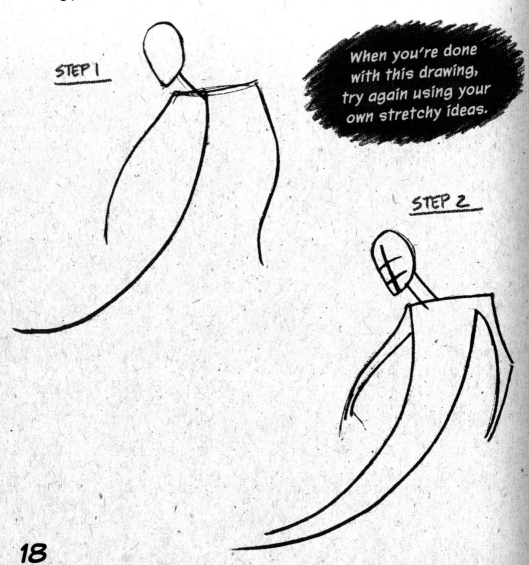

STEP I

When you're done with this drawing, try again using your own stretchy ideas.

STEP 2

STEP 3

STEP 4

FINAL!

19

THUNDERFIST

Tired of being small and weak, Carl created a chemical formula to make him strong. Now he's called Thunderfist, and he can rip through concrete like it was cardboard. No crook can hide from this mountain of muscle!

STEP 1

After practicing this drawing, try showing Thunderfist blasting his way through a brick wall!

STEP 2

STEP 3.

STEP 4

FINAL!

21

THE CREATURE

When criminals are on the loose, The Creature goes to work! His snarling face strikes fear into the hearts of criminals far and wide. When he's on the hunt, thugs can't escape his super sense of smell and tireless strength.

STEP 1

When you're done with this drawing, try showing The Creature sniffing out a big-time crook!

STEP 2

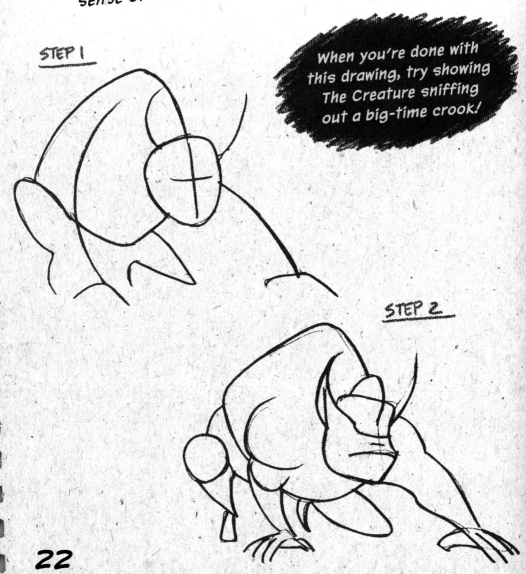

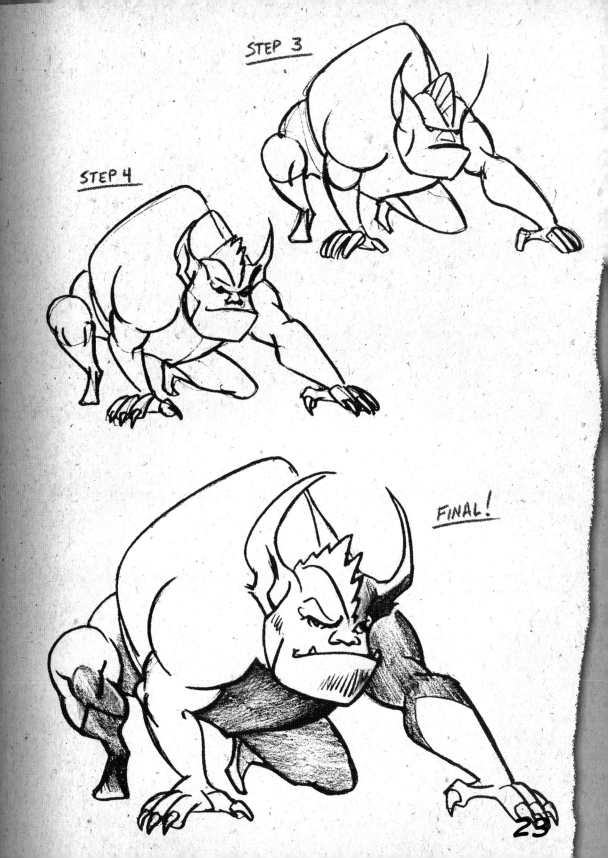

STEP 3

STEP 4

FINAL!

25

CAPTAIN ATMO

Captain Atmo is the world's most powerful hero. He's more than a mile tall and can pulverize mountains with his sonic fist blast. Whenever giant asteroids or alien ships threaten Earth, Captain Atmo is on the job!

After you've practiced this drawing, try showing Captain Atmo smashing an asteroid above the Earth!

STEP 1

STEP 2

STEP 3

STEP 4

FINAL!

25

DRAGONFLY

Joe was a simple pilot dusting crops one day when his plane crashed. He survived, but he was soaked in chemicals. The next day he woke up with an extra pair of arms, superhuman strength, and he could run at incredible speeds. Now Joe fights crime as the world's newest hero—Dragonfly!

STEP 1

When you've finished this drawing, try showing Dragonfly chasing down some crooks!

STEP 2

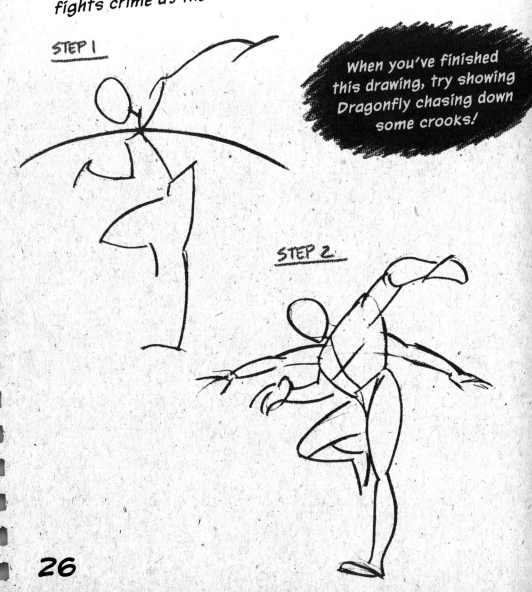

STEP 3

STEP 4

FINAL!

27

BLAZE

Most people can't lift cars over their heads. But it's easy for Blaze. A freak accident at a power plant gave her super strength and the ability to travel through power lines. She can appear anywhere an electrical outlet is found. Criminals know to be on the lookout for this shocking hero!

After you've practiced this drawing, try giving Blaze some thugs to take down in a fight!

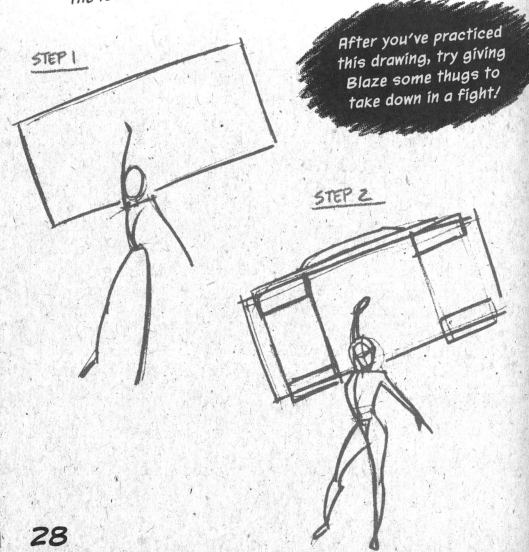

STEP 1

STEP 2

28

STEP 3

STEP 4

FINAL!

29

GLOSSARY

chemical (KEM-uh-kuhl)—a substance that creates a reaction

criminal (KRIM-uh-nuhl)—someone who commits a crime

formula (FOR-myuh-luh)—a combination of chemicals used to change something

indestructible (in-di-STRUHK-tuh-buhl)—something that can't be destroyed

power plant (POW-ur PLANT)—a building or group of buildings used to create electricity

pulverize (PUHL-vuh-rize)—to smash to bits

sonic (SON-ik)—having to do with sound waves

teleport (TELL-uh-port)—to transport oneself by instantly disappearing from one location and reappearing in another

thug (THUHG)—a violent criminal

READ MORE

Behling, Steve. *How to Draw X-Men*. How to Draw. New York: Scholastic, 2003.

Jurgens, Dan. *Marvel Characters*. You Can Draw. New York: DK Publishing, 2006.

Okum, David. *Draw Super Heroes!* Cincinnati: Impact, 2005.

INTERNET SITES

FactHound offers a safe, fun way to find Internet sites related to this book. All of the sites on FactHound have been researched by our staff.

Here's how:
1. Visit *www.facthound.com*
2. Choose your grade level.
3. Type in this book ID code **1429600748** for age-appropriate sites. You may also browse subjects by clicking on letters, or by clicking on pictures and words.
4. Click on the **Fetch It** button.

FactHound will fetch the best sites for you!

INDEX